SUNBIRD
PUBLISHING

First published 2000
2 4 6 8 10 9 7 5 3 1
Sunbird Publishing (Pty) Ltd
34 Sunset Avenue, Llandudno, Cape Town, South Africa
Registration number: 4850177827

Publisher Dick Wilkins
Editor Sean Fraser
Designer Mandy McKay
Production Manager Andrew de Kock

Reproduction by Unifoto (Pty) Ltd, Cape Town
Printed and bound by Tien Wah Press (Pte) Ltd, Singapore

ISBN 0-624-03887-4

*For Marc and Gilly Schwitter, Ian Clark, Deon and Crystal Cuyler,
and all our other friends in Botswana*

The gemsbok has evolved to conquer the harsh Kalahari environment.

...ivious to the flaming sky painting everything it touches, lions

...a rain-filled pan in Santawani, Okavango Delta.

...ck of red-billed queleas swarm between water and trees alongside

...ver in the Delta.

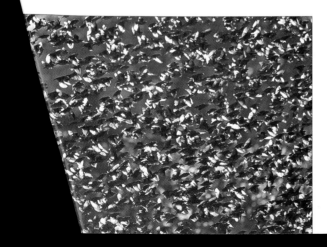

WILD
BOTSWANA

Introducing Botswana

Botswana is the Cinderella of the African continent. From rags to riches – with the discovery of diamonds in 1967 – the country turned from the poor relative into one of the richest nations in Africa almost at the wave of a wand. This stroke of good fortune coincided with independence from British protection when the new government had little more than a stable cattle industry on which to rely. Today, diamond earnings have eclipsed beef exports and, although diamonds might be an economy's best friend, Botswana's true wealth lies in its wilderness.

Most of the country is covered by pavement-coloured Kalahari sand, and yet it remains seductively attractive.

BELOW Sir Laurens van der Post described the Tsodilo Hills as the 'Louvre of the desert'. This panel of rock art on the Male Hill is named after him.

Much of the vegetation thrives in the sand, which – together with a little annual rain – upgrades the geographic status of the region from desert to semiarid. With scarce resources and poor agricultural potential, the Kalahari cannot sustain huge numbers of people or animals. These constraints have spared the nation from the industrial, agricultural and human onslaught that has overrun the rest of the developing world. A sizeable chunk of the country has been set aside as protected wilderness – so much so that a national park or game reserve occupies nearly every corner of Botswana.

The Central Kalahari Game Reserve is one of the world's largest, and was originally proclaimed to preserve the hunter-gatherer lifestyle of the Basarwa people whose livelihood depended on the ability to roam and live off the land. Few of these nomadic desert people remain today and the protection of the wilderness has now become the priority of the reserve.

Although there are signposts and artificial water holes and a scattering of dusty villages in the vicinity, the Central Kalahari Game Reserve has an unshakeable aura of remoteness. This atmosphere is heightened by the quivering wail of a jackal at sunset, galvanising his kind into a haunting chorus of howls. Regal black-maned lions prowl the sands of the reserve and, as night falls, their deep bellows strike fear into the hearts of the vulnerable. Antelope huddle together, humans throw more wood on the fire, while nervous travellers turn in for the night and fervently fasten their tents.

This is big-sky country. On moonless nights, the vastness of the sky is impossible to comprehend and when the moon is full you can read by its light. By day, the Kalahari has no horizon: only weathered camelthorn trees, fossil riverbeds, and gentle dunes ease the monotony of the flat countryside.

ABOVE As dusk falls, an impala mother gently grooms her lamb.

The town of Ghanzi owes its existence to the nearby limestone ridge with a bountiful underground water supply. Ghanzi's documented history began with the occupation by Afrikaner farmers in the 1870s. In time, the settlers were allocated large pieces of land upon which a tentative cattle industry was raised – and still flourishes. The town recently bolted to prominence with the completion of the Trans-Kgalagadi highway linking Namibia to Mozambique via Botswana and South Africa. As a result, Ghanzi now presents weary travellers with a smattering of civilisation.

South of the Central Kalahari Game Reserve lies the Kgalagadi Transfrontier Park, Africa's first international game reserve. The park spans South Africa and Botswana and is administered jointly by both countries. Animals migrate freely between the two countries, oblivious to immigration formalities and artificial boundaries. The southern Kalahari landscape is much the same as its northern neighbour, but serviced camp sites and graded roads render the Kgalagadi Transfrontier Park more charitable to tourists.

Here cheetah families hunt in ancient riverbeds where springbok herds strut proudly as if in defiance of their desolate surroundings. Camelthorn trees languish under the thatch tenements of sociable weavers, and the huge haystacks of interwoven grass provide shelter to hundreds of these small birds. As the flock grows, more extensions are added and the weight of the nest can become insupportable, and it is not uncommon for the host tree to suddenly lose the limb supporting the nest.

Below Shortly after the rains begin to fall, an explosion of fireball lilies erupts alongside luminous shoots of fresh grass.

Kalahari conditions are extreme. Summer swelters at 40°C and winter freezes to minus 11°C. Ravaged by dust blizzards in the dry season and violent thunderstorms in the wet, the land is at the mercy of the elements. But when the rains do come, the Kalahari responds dramatically, spawning seed and lamb, chick and tadpole. Few complain about this season of plenty. Then, all too soon, it passes and life returns to the world of drought, heat and dust.

A feast of tales recounts the tragic fate of adventurers and geologists who underestimated the tyranny of the desert, but the Kalahari's animals have evolved the skills to survive. Although graceful gemsbok seem to dominate the reserve's water holes, they seldom need to actually drink water, obtaining moisture from the plants they eat. They are able to prevent themselves from sweating to retain water and boast a fancy physiological adaptation that prevents their brains from overheating. When summer's heat is at its zenith, ground squirrels arch their enormous fluffy tails over their heads as umbrellas and, on icy winter mornings, suricate families huddle together for warmth to save both energy and heat.

The hundreds of salt pans found in the far eastern corner of Kgalagadi are familiar features of Botswana's landscape, and the salt-encrusted depressions remain as evidence that most of Botswana once foundered under a giant inland sea until seismic disturbances caused the tide to go out and never return. When summer rains fall, the pans collect sheets of milky water, storing it long into winter when the sands have swallowed all other evidence of surface moisture. This way, pans provide a lifeline for creatures of a water-poor country.

The largest of all Botswana's pans, the Makgadikgadi Pans extend for 12 000 square kilometres and comprise two major pans – Sowa and Ntwetwe. This expanse of bleached emptiness that stretches beyond the limits of the horizon – and the imagination – is both surreal and beautiful. The rains entice miniature crustaceans out of their underground nursery, providing a harvest to the thousands of water birds

Above Marabou stork chicks nest on a fig tree island on an Okavango lagoon.

that migrate to the area. Sowa Pan is particularly popular with greater flamingoes and is the biggest breeding ground for these birds in Africa. One local community has established the Nata Sanctuary, where an elevated viewing platform offers one of the best views of the pan, and the homely Nata Lodge, a short drive from the sanctuary, has accommodated travellers to these parts for over 14 years.

West of Ntwetwe Pan, the Makgadikgadi Pans National Park preserves vast meadows of grassland, which draw animals into the region in the wet season. The grasses are nutritious to domestic animals too and Khumaga camp is regularly overrun with cattle and goats from the nearby village.

Nxai Pan also enjoys these awesome seasonal migrations, but is perhaps more famous for its stand of 'upside-down giants' immortalised in the paintings of Thomas Baines. Baine's Baobabs, an island of seven baobab trees surrounded by a sea of pale sand, is one of the most engaging sights in Botswana. The trees are perfectly aligned for mesmerising sunsets and provide a vital landmark for moonlit strolls.

When the pans dry out and the promise of rain is still months away, the country looks north to its only two permanent water features to sustain it – the Okavango Delta and the Chobe River.

The Delta traces its roots to the Angolan mountains from where the Kavango River travels south, intent on reaching the sea. The parent river flows energetically into Botswana from Namibia, before suddenly spawning wayward streams that take off in all directions, assuming the shape of a rough triangle. This is the lush Okavango Delta, home to a fascinating assembly of people, birds, fish and animals. The water, however, never makes it to the sea as the sun, sand and thirsty plants conspire to exhaust the Delta's energy and its journey expires in Botswana's Ngamiland province.

It is a remarkable sight where desert becomes delta: scrubland makes way for towering riverine forests and tropical palms supplant hardy thorn trees; languid waters

BELOW Even with its bulk completely submerged, the small ears, piggy eyes and hairy nostrils are a dead give-away for this hippopotamus.

crowded with papyrus heads nodding in the breeze mock the parched sands and dusty wasteland. It is here that ancient men swapped bows and arrows for fishing traps and *mokoros* as water became the dominant medium.

The *mokoro* is the king of the Delta's waterways. It is the primary means of water transport and plays taxi, cargo carrier, fishing boat and even tourist joyride. Hewn from the stem of mature marula, jackalberry or sausage trees – concern about the unsustainable use of the Delta's ancient trees has created a demand for fibreglass imitations of the *mokoro* – the wooden boats have a life span of about five years.

Descendants of the Delta's early inhabitants still live in its northern reaches, in an area called the Panhandle after its shape on the map. The Panhandle is a microcosm of traditional Delta living where the land is generous to its tenants. Villages are constructed from materials on hand, such as thatch, mud and reeds. Giant fishing baskets are woven from dry grass, and chickens flap in the dust around the villages, providing variety to a diet dominated by fish.

Fishing poles and nets increasingly replace the traditional baskets and the activity has taken on an economic rather than subsistence aspect. Basket-weaving is, however, still a practised skill among the Hambukushu women of the Delta, and their handiwork is displayed in a basket shop at a village called Etsha 6, one of 13 Etsha communities settled by Hambukushu refugees fleeing war-torn Angola decades ago.

Moving west from the Panhandle, the featureless terrain resumes – until a rocky outcrop on the horizon takes on a significance of supernatural proportions. These are the four Tsodilo Hills, spiritual home to several of Botswana's tribes. The Hambukushu people believe their god lowered them and their cattle onto the largest hill at the beginning of time, while San (Bushmen) lore holds that the gods are resident in the Hills and no creature must be killed in the vicinity or the gods will be angered and will punish the perpetrators. Even for nonbelievers the Hills have an eerie presence.

ABOVE Tourists enjoy a sunset cruise along the Chobe River.

For Tsodilo's early inhabitants, the Hills were a magnificent canvas upon which to practice their art, leading one commentator to hail Tsodilo as the 'Louvre of the desert'. Paintings of rhinoceros, giraffe and eland grace the rocks, hinting at a time when wildlife roamed the countryside where cattle and donkeys now graze.

Moremi Game Reserve protects almost one third of the Okavango Delta and its wild inhabitants. Luxury lodges and stylish mobile safaris cater for the swarms of visitors to the reserve. Lion, leopard, cheetah and wild dog collaborate to entertain spectators in open-topped vehicles, while hippo and crocodile thrill tourists in motorboats or *mokoros*.

But most beguiling of all is the bird life. Specials such as Pel's fishing owls and slaty egrets are there for the ticking, and every duck, goose and teal imaginable seems to float on the waters of the Delta. The reeds and puddles are alive with storks and waders, and an album of birdsong compiled by woodland kingfishers and doves plays all day, bravely competing with the cackles of francolins and babblers.

Maun, the gateway to the Okavango, is clearly the heart of the safari industry: khaki gear, designer pen knives and battered 4x4s are the most conspicuous icons of this vibrant town. In the restaurants and bars, bush pilots and safari guides regale with stories of adventure and daring. In years of good Okavango floods, the Thamalakane River trickles through the town, bringing in the odd hippopotamus as well as a buzz to the littered streets.

Kasane is a riverside town not unlike Maun, except here the khaki-clad wildlife enthusiasts head for Chobe National Park on the edge of town. The park takes its name from the Chobe River, which forms the northern boundary of the reserve, and is most famous for its elephants. From the droves of breeding herds on the riverfront to the gentle old bulls in Savute, from the Linyanti swamps to the woodlands of Nogaatsa and Tchinga, Chobe is elephant nirvana. Leisure boats patrol the great river at sunset when the elephants

BELOW The psychedelic lilac-breasted roller is Botswana's national bird.

come down to drink and swim, and these gentle giants perform the same scene in the Linyanti wetlands, a mini Okavango in the northwestern reaches of the park. In the Savute region, safari vehicles stop at Pump Pan, an artificially pumped water hole, to watch mild-natured bulls shuffle past the cars and quietly bully each other over drinking space.

In summer, the elephants evaporate into the woodlands and thousands of zebras arrive to steal the show. Lured by the scent of fresh new grass the zebras trek in their droves from their winter refuge along the river banks of the Linyanti, stopping over on the Savute Marsh before making for the lush grazing in Mababe further south. As the rain-filled pans vaporise and the dry season looms, they gather again for the long return journey. In time, the elephants abandon the woodlands and wander back to the water holes – and so the rhythm of wet and dry, coming and going, continues.

Botswana's elephant population is equally at home in Tuli Block in the far east of the country. Here Mashatu Game Reserve holds the record for the most elephants roaming private land. Mashatu's breeding herds are uncharacteristically tolerant of visitors and it is not uncommon to find a vehicle surrounded by an entire family of elephants of all ages solely intent on eating every blade or leaf in sight.

This eastern corridor of Botswana is the only part of the country that is not smothered by Kalahari sand. In stark contrast to the prosaic Kalahari, the terrain is characterised by rocky outcrops, giant nyala trees and wild sesame bushes. The network of seasonal rivers that crisscross the landscape has made life much gentler here and most of Botswana's human population has settled in the area.

Gaborone was declared the capital city with independence in 1966, and has all the trappings of a flourishing city – high-rise buildings, a museum, art gallery and university, as well as rush hour traffic – but several game reserves just outside the city limits are a reminder of the wilderness not far from the doorstep.

ABOVE A herd of cattle treks through Kalahari grasslands.

Francistown, Botswana's oldest and second-largest city, is a bustling metropolis of modern malls and fast-food outlets, although few visitors need venture beyond the lush grounds of the Marang Motel on the banks of the Tati River. The city has its origins in the gold rush of the late 19th century and takes its name from Daniel Francis, an English prospector. Few mines still operate in Francistown, but other industries sustain it as the economic hub of the country.

Botswana continues as a yardstick for the rest of the continent, and the country has managed to adopt Western ideals without sacrificing its own traditional heritage. *Kgotlas*, or community assemblies, typically situated under a prominent tree in the village, are as vital as the country's highest courts to the judicial and administrative life of Botswana's citizens. And the House of Chiefs, representing the nation's main tribal groupings, plays an integral role in the legislature. But it is Botswana's handling of its natural heritage that deserves the loudest applause. At the beginning of the 21st century, this small landlocked state is custodian to an asset that so many other countries have irretrievably squandered – a vast and revered wilderness.

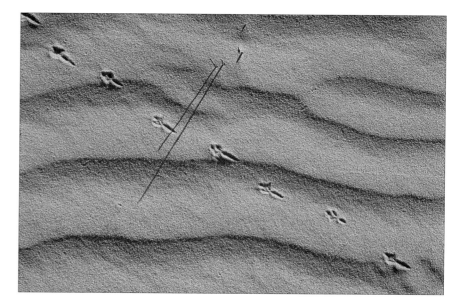

LEFT AND ABOVE Most of Botswana is built on layers of fine Kalahari sand. The wind only temporarily dusts all signs from the ground – before long, even the most light-footed visitor will leave its mark.

OPPOSITE A lone springbok ram grazes in the dust in Deception Valley, a relic riverbed in the Central Kalahari Game Reserve.

LEFT AND OPPOSITE King of all he surveys. The Kalahari is famous for its regal black-maned lions. The mane is usually fully grown when the lion reaches five years of age, although there are records of adult males that have no mane at all.

BELOW The scraggly mane on this young male suggests he still has some growing up to do.

LEFT A thunderstorm looms over the Nossob riverbed, a natural boundary between Botswana and South Africa in the Kgalagadi Transfrontier Park. Here, the animals enjoy diplomatic immunity as they wander freely between the two countries in Africa's pioneer international game reserve.

RIGHT A blazing campfire keeps away the desert cold – and the lions – at this remote Kalahari camp site.

OPPOSITE A sunset is enhanced by the innocuous pollution of dust and evaporated water that has filtered the evening sky.

LEFT Cheetah are regularly seen in the Kalahari reserves, but prove to be more elusive in other parts of the country.

ABOVE Dramatic chases such as this are often witnessed by visitors in the middle of the day, when cheetah – unlike most other cats – prefer to hunt.

OPPOSITE A mother cheetah and her four cubs slake their thirst at an artificial water hole in the Kgalagadi Transfrontier Park.

OVERLEAF Two of the Kalahari's most furtive cats, the African wild cat (*left*) and the leopard (*right*).

ABOVE At the entrance to their burrow, an inquisitive Cape fox pup inspects its mother while she waits for the sun to set.

LEFT The versatility of black-backed jackals enables them to live in just about any environment. In the Kalahari, they often tail cheetahs in the hope of snatching a morsel after a kill.

OPPOSITE Ground squirrels warm themselves in the winter morning sun after a characteristically freezing Kalahari night.

LEFT As the moon rises over a camelthorn tree, stargazing opportunities fade. On moonless nights, the infinity of the galaxy is overwhelming.

OPPOSITE A herd of gemsbok is dwarfed by the omnipotence of an oncoming storm. Such tempestuous Kalahari downpours are usually mercifully brief.

RIGHT Summer rains transform the thirstland into a lush garden, with a feast of sweet grazing for these springbok. In years of good rain, the Kalahari's fossil riverbeds are revived and the rivers begin to flow once again, albeit for just a short period.

LEFT A bateleur surveys its surrounds for any flurry of movement that might be a meal.

ABOVE A lanner falcon celebrates the unexpected bounty of a grasshopper eruption and homes in on a hapless individual.

OPPOSITE Two pygmy falcons haggle over a sociable weaver chick. These petite raptors are frequently uninvited houseguests in the giant communal nests of sociable weavers and are not above pilfering their host's offspring from the nursery.

LEFT AND ABOVE Ever alert, a ground squirrel (*left*) and suricate (*above*) on sentry duty.
OPPOSITE A 360-degree look-out declares the area free of lurking predators, and safe
for other suricates to emerge from the burrow.

LEFT Exceptionally well adapted to desert conditions, gemsbok can reportedly survive without drinking water, obtaining all the moisture they need from desert plants such as tsamma melons. Yet, when water is available, they make the most of it and are frequently seen at water holes in the Kalahari.

BELOW AND OPPOSITE It is believed that the gemsbok is responsible for the origins of the mythical one-horned unicorn. Viewed at an appropriate angle from the side, the rapier horns merge into one and the animal bears an eerie resemblance to its fairytale caricature.

OVERLEAF LEFT The wet season transforms the desolate Makgadikgadi landscape into a watery paradise, drawing thousands of migrant birds such as these red-billed teals.

OVERLEAF RIGHT A herd of impala starts its day at Nxai Pan, the only wild place in Botswana where springbok and impala occur together.

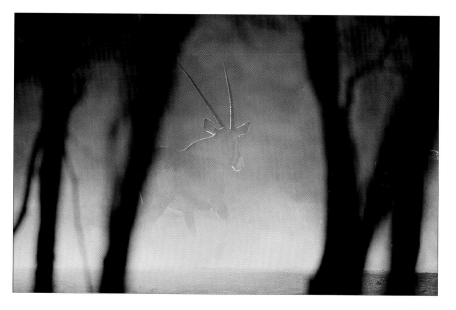

PREVIOUS PAGES AND ABOVE The grasslands bordering the Makgadikgadi Pans attract thousands of zebra in the wet season. As they march through the pans, their footprints linger in the soft clay as evidence of their visit long after they have passed.

LEFT The small forest of baobabs named after artist Thomas Baines dominates the white expanse of Kudiakam Pan.

OPPOSITE At night, the palm trees imitate the sound of falling rain as their leaves rustle in the wind and fooled visitors wake up to a bone-dry Makgadikgadi.

OVERLEAF LEFT A young lion, with all the clumsiness of its unskilled youth, hones its stalking technique in the grasslands at Nxai Pan.

OVERLEAF RIGHT Capped wheat-ear chicks perch atop their termite-mound nest and demand food from their mother.

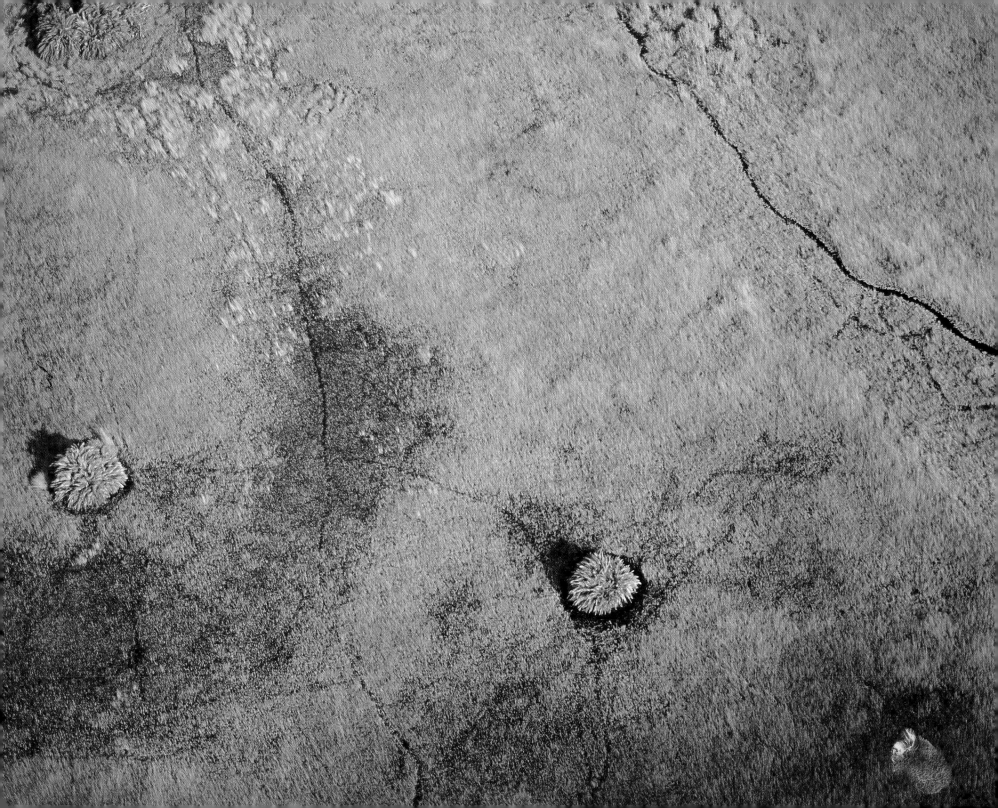

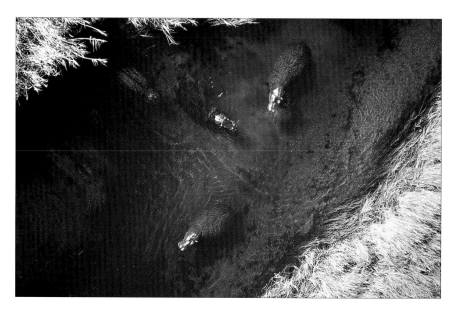

PREVIOUS PAGE LEFT Guides pole tourists in dugout canoes – called *mokoros* – through the web of channels that make up the Okavango Delta.

PREVIOUS PAGE RIGHT An aerial view of a patch of the Delta shows the trails cleared by hippos, which is how many of the channels are formed.

LEFT A small herd of buffalo makes its way through the grasslands of Chief's Island – at 1 000 square kilometres, the largest island in the Okavango Delta.

ABOVE The clear tea-coloured waters of the Delta fail to conceal this pod of hippos from the eyes in the sky.

OPPOSITE Swishing tails as if in affront to the aerial disturbance, a herd of giraffe canters gracefully across the landscape of Chief's Island.

OPPOSITE Fishermen in a traditional *mokoro* check their nets for the day's catch.
OVERLEAF LEFT 'He who pushes his *ingushi* (pole) too deep, stays with it,' goes the warning to novice polers. Where the waters run deep, long paddles are used in place of poles to manoeuvre the *mokoro*.
OVERLEAF RIGHT A deep, wide channel snakes through fields of papyrus, clearing the path for a charging motor boat.

ABOVE A palm tree island rises up out of the watery meadows of the Delta.
RIGHT Tourism has transformed the once-sprawling village of Maun into the bustling capital of Botswana's safari industry.

LEFT AND ABOVE Zebras in Botswana always seem to be on the move, following the rain and lush grazing that it brings. The permanent fresh water and sweet grass of the Delta appeal to the more sedentary zebras.

OPPOSITE Botswana is famous throughout Africa and, indeed, the world, for its vast free-ranging herds of elephant.

OVERLEAF LEFT A towering riverine forest broods over impalas frolicking across a flood plain.

OVERLEAF RIGHT At war over territory, red lechwe males chase each other through the shallows. During these feuds, the males lock horns and wrestle until a victor finally emerges.

The Okavango Delta is a magnet for more than 400 bird species. Fluttering in the skies, perched in the trees, wading in the pools or paddling in the deep, there's hardly a square metre unoccupied by these feathered creatures, among them the coppery-tailed coucal (*top left*), African skimmer (*left*), carmine bee-eater (*above*) and Egyptian goose (*opposite*). The frequent arrival of migrants augment the ranks and add new voices to the soundtrack of birdsong that plays day and night.

OVERLEAF LEFT Thousands of small islands such as these float in the Okavango Delta and provide vital dry land environments to a variety of birds and wild animals.

OVERLEAF RIGHT Tiny malachite kingfishers boast a full spectrum of colours in their plumage. Papyrus stalks provide an ideal perch from which to dive-bomb the Delta's fish life.

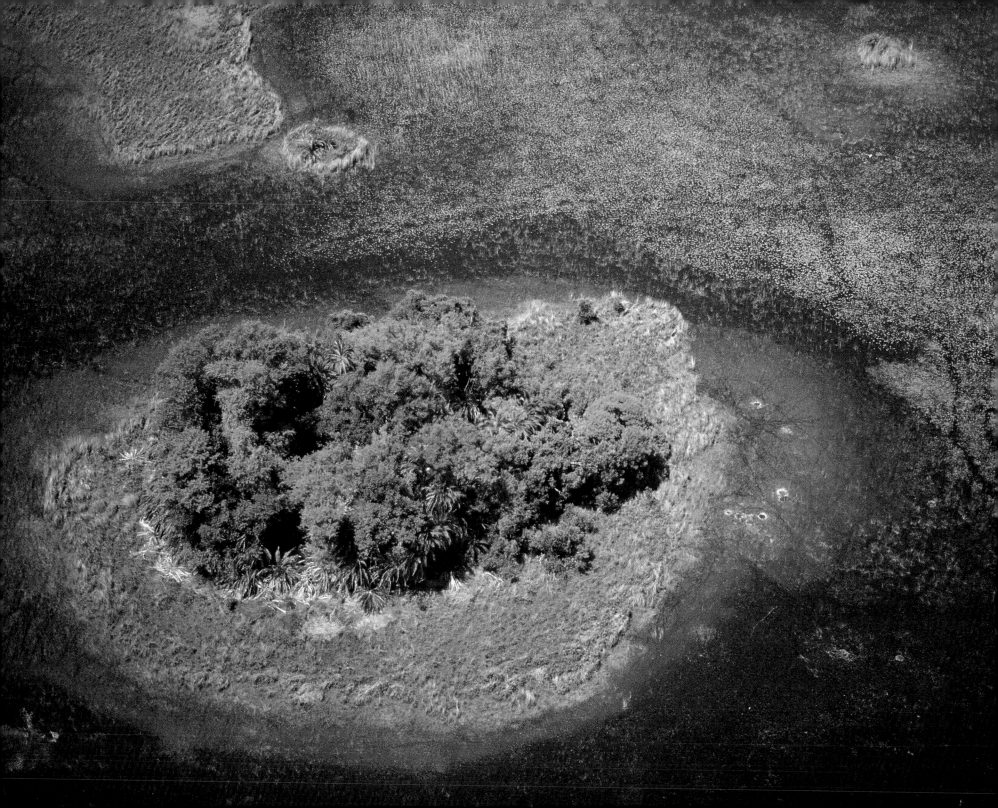

ABOVE AND ABOVE RIGHT A potpourri of long-legged birds favour the water's edge as a suitable feeding area, among them the painted snipe (*above*) and the black-winged stilt (*above right*).

OPPOSITE African jacanas are entirely at home on the Okavango Delta's lily pads upon which they regularly nest.

LEFT Before the Okavango River spills into the Delta, it runs deep and fast through a region known as the Panhandle, leaving steep river banks in its wake. Around September each year, flocks of migrant carmine bee-eaters excavate tunnels in the river banks and begin a frenzy of breeding.

ABOVE Wild date palms fringe this Delta island. The only other palm that grows in the Okavango is the real fan palm, which can reach an impressive height of some 20 metres – compared to the six-metre stretch of its shorter companion.

OPPOSITE A patchwork quilt of flooded grasslands, palm tree islands and meandering channels stretches beyond the horizon.

ABOVE A little bittern skulks in the dense growth of a papyrus stand.
ABOVE RIGHT A saddle-billed stork scrutinises the shallows for stranded fish in a drying pool.

OPPOSITE A frequent visitor to the flood plains of the Okavango Delta, a ruff baths in a rain-water pan near the Third Bridge camp site.

LEFT AND TOP Large numbers of African wild dogs once roamed the continent. Today, the Okavango Delta is one of the last refuges for this critically endangered species.

ABOVE A playful young wild dog takes on a herd of wildebeest. Although wild dogs hunt wildebeest in East Africa, impala and other medium-sized antelope are the dogs' prey of choice in Botswana.

OPPOSITE Popular myth holds that wild dogs are cruel killers that will even eat their own kind. In reality, the pack is a complex social structure in which sick or injured dogs are fed and cared for by its other members. They generally also dispatch their prey much quicker than any other predator.

PREVIOUS PAGE LEFT Giraffe and zebra gather to drink from the Khwai River – the easternmost finger of the Okavango Delta.

PREVIOUS PAGE RIGHT A leopard, draped over the bough of a weathered camelthorn tree, soaks up the last rays of sunlight before night settles.

LEFT, ABOVE AND OPPOSITE In the late afternoon, lionesses and cubs alike start to shake off the day's long slumber and contemplate a night of hunting.

OVERLEAF LEFT In the wet season, elephants in Moremi Game Reserve abandon the forest in favour of the lush new grasses carpeting Gamdzabu Plain.

OVERLEAF RIGHT Cattle egrets roost in the skeletons of drowned trees in Moremi Game Reserve.

LEFT A movement in the long grass, a sound or a scent carried on the wind, alerts this impala ram to potential danger.

ABOVE Red lechwe snort in alarm and prepare to run as a stalking lion is detected.

OPPOSITE A herd of wildebeest closes ranks as night and its attendant predators advance.

ABOVE When the trees are brimming with spring's bounty some animals will go to great lengths to get to the flowers. Here, a kudu strains its tongue for a dainty blossom.
ABOVE RIGHT An impala makes short work of a flower from a sausage tree.

OPPOSITE True to their name, waterbuck – easily identified by the circular marking on the rump – are always found close to water as they are unable to survive for more than a couple of days without drinking.

LEFT, FROM TOP TO BOTTOM The Delta ecosystem is well suited to aquatic antelope such as the red lechwe. Elongated, splayed hooves and powerful back legs allow them to run at considerable speed through the water.

ABOVE In the mating season, courtship rituals regularly involve a high-speed chase through water for the eager suitor and the reluctant object of his desire.

OPPOSITE Red lechwe usually feed in the flooded grasslands, standing belly-deep in the water.

LEFT At Popa Falls, the Okavango River trips over a ridge of boulders before leaving Namibia for the Botswana leg of its long journey.

ABOVE The sun sets over a languid Okavango River near Shakawe.

OPPOSITE Spur-winged geese saunter toward the water on a misty Okavango morning.

OVERLEAF LEFT Giraffe amble across a windswept Savute Marsh in Chobe National Park.

OVERLEAF RIGHT Huge herds of buffalo kick up dust as they converge on the Chobe River during the dry season.

LEFT, ABOVE AND OPPOSITE More than anything, elephants love to bathe. When the rainy season dumps water in Savute's pans, elephants take to these pools with much enthusiasm. The swim is often followed by a mud spray and a dust shower.

OVERLEAF Warthog (*left*) and wildebeest (*right*) both get down on their knees to drink. In this position, the wildebeest is particularly vulnerable to predators and will only take the decision to kneel after a painstakingly tedious survey of its surroundings.

OVERLEAF LEFT So much grass, so little time. An elephant wallows in the long grass upholstering Savute Marsh in the wet season.
OVERLEAF RIGHT Pumped water holes like Marabou Pan sustain Savute's resident bull elephants during the long, dry season.

ABOVE, RIGHT AND OPPOSITE At the first sign of summer rain, thousands of zebra leave their winter refuge along the banks of the Linyanti River in Chobe National Park and head for the sweet grasses of the Mababe Depression. Here they socialise, breed and nurture their young until the pans begin to dry and the signs of autumn drive them back along the 500-kilometre route.

TOP LEFT At the close of day, elephants near the Chobe River continue eating, digging up juicy roots with their heavy feet.

LEFT Savute's elephants make their way to the water holes where they jostle for vital sips of water. In the height of the dry season, it is not uncommon to see 30 elephants bullying each other around the small pans.

ABOVE One of a number of baobab trees that are prominent features of the Savute landscape. This baobab is a favourite sundowner site for visitors on game drives.

OPPOSITE A game-viewing vehicle finds itself surrounded by hundreds of buffalo as the herd wanders back to the shelter of the woodlands after drinking from the Chobe River at dawn.

OVERLEAF LEFT Back-to-back, two impala rams are wary of the potential dangers hidden by the soft light and long grass.

OVERLEAF RIGHT A herd of waterbuck gathers near the water's edge on Sidudu Island in the Chobe River.

LEFT The neck of an impala ram, stooped to drink, is as good a perch as any for this red-billed oxpecker, which pecks away at parasites on the antelope's body.

ABOVE AND OPPOSITE LEFT When the elephants relinquish control over Savute's Pump Pan, a horde of animals, such as these kudu ewes (*above*) and kudu bull (*opposite left*), streams in to snatch a quick sip.

OPPOSITE RIGHT Steenbok are shy animals and are usually only noticed when the frightened animal is leaping and bounding away. Perhaps the tasty browsing helped this steenbok overcome bashfulness.

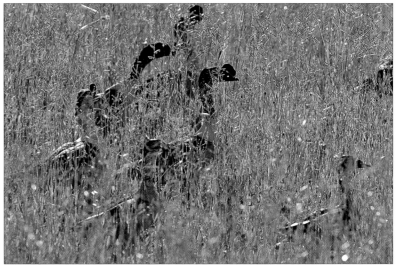

PREVIOUS PAGES Summer birding in Savute is spectacular. Thousands of migrant birds, including Abdim's storks, flock to the pans and puddles where they feed on the eruptions of insects and other creatures that emerge after the rains.

LEFT Red-billed francolins are Chobe's avian alarm clocks, announcing the break of day long before the sun even rises to herald the morning.

ABOVE Knob-billed ducks migrate to Chobe National Park in summer where they march through the grasslands in crews, harvesting seeds from the tips of the grasses.

OPPOSITE Savute's visiting carmine bee-eaters have adopted the comical habit of riding on the backs of unperturbed kori bustards to hawk the insects disturbed by the big bird's progress.

PREVIOUS PAGE LEFT Grotesque limbs of drowned trees create a ghostly backdrop for a herd of nervous impala.

PREVIOUS PAGE RIGHT A leopard is a rare sight, even here on the appropriately named Leopard Rock, one of seven hills rising out of the flat Savute landscape.

THESE PAGES When the dry season is at its zenith, all manner of birds, such these helmeted guineafowl (*left*), blue-cheecked bee-eaters (*top*), yellow-billed kites (*above*) and Burchell's sandgrouse (*opposite*), rush to the meagre and crowded water sources, risking life and wing for a vital sip of water.

PREVIOUS PAGE LEFT A typical gathering of animals at Pump Pan during the searing heat of the unavailing dry season.

PREVIOUS PAGE RIGHT Although hippos prefer to spend most of the day submerged in water and emerge to graze at night, they are commonly seen on the banks of the Chobe River.

TOP LEFT Nemesis of the lion and maligned object of myth, the hyena, like the wild dog, suffers from a bad public image, fuelled by a poor understanding of its behaviour and intricate social structure.

LEFT A dead elephant is like a giant grey pantry and will feed these hyenas and their cubs for several days. Contrary to their reputation as cowardly scavengers, hyenas are able hunters and regularly bring down their own prey.

ABOVE An aardwolf mother and cub emerge from their den on the Savute Marsh as the promise of night-time cover approaches.

OPPOSITE A black-backed jackal gets its paws wet in order to slake its thirst in the water.

LEFT AND BELOW The lions of Savute have had more than their 15 minutes of fame in the popular film and television documentaries of their lives. Not long ago, a few of the larger prides made elephant hunting their speciality.

OPPOSITE A flehmen display by a male lion tests the scent of a nearby female in oestrus.

LEFT In the heat of the day, a lioness struggles to move a wildebeest carcass to the shade some distance away.

TOP AND ABOVE This is the substance of most lion sightings – drowsy cats paying little attention to the activity around them.

OPPOSITE When a zebra foal strays from the herd death is a certainty.

PREVIOUS PAGES A colourful explosion of wild flowers adorns the Tuli landscape in eastern Botswana.

LEFT A board used in the age-old African game of *marabaraba* is one of the relics found at the Mmamagwe archeological site in Mashatu Game Reserve.

ABOVE A cheetah scans the horizon for potential prey.

OPPOSITE The flowers of the devil's thorn prove irresistible to this herd of elephant, their trunks stained yellow from the pollen. Mashatu's breeding herds are remarkably mild in nature and regularly tolerate game-drive vehicles in close proximity.

LEFT Mashatu is no stranger to helmeted guineafowl scratching for food in the rustling grasses.
ABOVE Bicycle safaris are unique to Mashatu Game Reserve. Armed rangers guide guests through the reserve, while a recovery vehicle trails at a distance to rescue the unfit.
OPPOSITE A startled flock of cattle egrets and wattled starlings takes to the safety of the sky.
OVERLEAF Night falls over Francistown, Botswana's oldest and second-largest city.

ACKNOWLEDGEMENTS

We did not specifically set out to compile this book; rather, it is the inevitable result of the past five years – much of which has been spent exploring this beguiling country. We would like to thank all those individuals who have contributed (some unwittingly) to the production of this book, among them Giles Badger, Rowland and Shirley-Ann Bailey, Megan Bailey and Frank Rees, Mosiako Bashe, Ralph Bousfield and Catherine Raphaely, David Bristow, Brent Dacomb, Jan, Eileen, Donovan and Lawrence Drotsky, Derek Flatt, Jonathan Gibson, Tony and Kimberly Hardwick, David Hartley, Murray Hibbs, Wayne and Venessa Hinde, Brad Horn, Brian and Elaine Keene-Young, Bronwyn Keene-Young, Leigh Kemp, Graeme Labe, Phillip Lategan, Stuart Mackay, Ryan, Joanne and Callum Maritz, Witness Masasa, Tico McNutt and Lesley Boggs, John Modeme, Alison Morphet, Grant Nel, Peter and Pauline Perlstein, Photo Access, Des Pretorius, Veronica Roodt, Lindy Scholtz, Marc van Mourik, Murray Weiner and Fiona Dorst, the Wilderness Dawning clan, Jenny Witstock and Greg Woodside, and Dick Wilkins, Mandy McKay, Sean Fraser and the staff of Sunbird Publishing.

In addition, we would like to thank the management, guides and staff of all the camps at which we have stayed over the years, and all the pilots who conveyed us across the country.

Finally, we would also like to thank the Office of the President and the Department of Wildlife and National Parks for granting us the privilege of pursuing various projects in Botswana.

ADRIAN BAILEY & ROBYN KEENE-YOUNG, JOHANNESBURG, MAY 2000

USEFUL ADDRESSES

Air Charter & Game-Viewing Flights, Mack Air, Private Bag 329, Maun, Botswana, telefax (+267) 66 0675, e-mail mack.air@info.bw

Helicopter Charter & Game-Viewing Flights, Wildlife Helicopters, Private Bag 161, Maun, Botswana, telefax (+267) 66 0664, e-mail wildhel@info.bw

Chief's Camp, Abercrombie & Kent, PO Box 782607, Sandton 2146, South Africa, tel. (+27 11) 781 0740, fax (+27 11) 781 2241, e-mail omaia@res-centre.co.za

Mobile Tours & Safaris, AfroVentures, Private Bag X27, Benmore 2010, South Africa, tel. (+27 11) 809 4300, fax (+27 11) 809 4514, e-mail jnb@afroventures.com

Sandibe and Nxabega, CC Africa, Private Bag x 27, Benmore 2010, South Africa, tel. (+27 11) 809 4300, fax: (+27 11) 809 4400, e-mail reservations@ccafrica.com

Drotsky's Cabins, PO Box 115, Shakawe, Botswana, tel. (+267) 67 5035, fax (+267) 67 5043

Chobe Game Lodge, Camp Moremi, Camp Okavango, Tsaro Elephant Lodge and Xugana Lodge, Desert & Delta Safaris, PO Box 130555, Bryanston 2021, South Africa, tel. (+27 11) 706 0862/3, fax (+27 11) 706 0864, e-mail chobe@fast.co.za

The Marang Hotel, PO Box 807, Francistown, Botswana, tel. (+267) 21 3991, fax (+267) 21 2130, e-mail marang@info.bw

Oddball's and Delta Camp, Okavango Tours & Safaris, PO Box 39, Maun, Botswana, tel. (+267) 66 0220, fax (+267) 66 0589, e-mail okavango@info.bw

Selinda Camp, Zibalianja and Walking Trails, Linyanti Explorations, PO Box 22, Kasane, Botswana, tel. (+267) 65 0505, fax (+267) 65 0352, e-mail selinda@info.bw

Mashatu Game Reserve, Rattray Reserves, PO Box 2575, Randburg 2125, South Africa, tel. (+27 11) 789 2677, fax (+27 11) 886 4382, e-mail jhb@malamala.com

Jack's Camp and Mobile Safaris, Unchartered Africa Safaris, PO Box 173, Francistown, Botswana, tel. (+267) 21 2277 / 20 3309, fax (+267) 21 3458, e-mail unchart@info.bw

Parks & Reserves Reservations Office, PO Box 20364, Boseja, Maun, Botswana, tel. (+267) 66 1265, fax (+267) 66 1264; or PO Box 131, Gaborone, Botswana, tel. (+267) 58 0774, fax (+267) 58 0775, e-mail dwnpbots@global.bw